First published 1998
Revised edition 2000 AD
This edition © Wooden Books 2005 AD

Published by Wooden Books Ltd.
12A High St, Glastonbury, Somerset

British Library Cataloguing in Publication Data
Tibbs, D.C.
Fairy Rhymes

A CIP catalogue record for this delightful book
is available from the British Library

ISBN 1 904263 35 6

Printed and bound in Great Britain
by The Cromwell Press,
Trowbridge, Wiltshire, UK.

fairy rhymes

by

Carol Tibbs

illustrated by

Fiona Hughes

In my garden

This garden is where the fairies live,
  Where they come from I don't know,
But I know about the lovely gifts they give
And the love the fairies' show.

  They all hold hands and dance a lot,
  They look after flowers and trees;
  They talk with the insects and play a lot
  And do whatever they please.

They like to talk to people like me
Because we need to understand
That wherever the fairies come to dwell
  There'll be flowers all over the land.

Fairy folk

It's hard for elves to live in smoke,
  And pixies like the woods;
They're shy and hide away from us,
Even when we're very good.

  Dwarves like all the things of Earth,
  The crystals in the ground ...
  Wherever there are crystals
  There'll be a dwarf around.

The little elves all dress in white,
They are the fairy toffs;
Smoke makes their clothes all dirty
And gives them nasty coughs.

There are fairy folk all round you,
They watch us all the while.
They tend our window boxes
And make us want to smile.

To see the fairies at your home
You only have to say ...
For wherever there are plants and flowers
The fairies come and play.

bots of legs

Oh little insect on the wall
    Please stay there and do not fall.
Waving all your legs around
Is just not healthy on the ground.

Scaredy people just like me
Do not like your legs you see.
Because you run so very fast
    I can't move quick to let you past.

Surprise surprise

A fairy stood on a big stone
    She'd seen upon the ground.
The stone it moved beneath her
And there wasn't any sound!

Suprised, the fairy jumped and cried
    "Oh let me down, please do!"

"Why certainly," said the tortoise.
    "I'd do anything for you!"

Parrot in the park

In the park today I saw
  A cage which held a big Macaw
With feathers all of red and blue.
She squawked quite loudly
As parrots do.

  And when the park is closed at night
  The fairies come with fairy lights
  And with her they talk and sing
  Which is a very happy thing.

She comes from far across the sea
And where it's very hot to be.
She doesn't like it when it's chilly,
And being in a cage is silly.

So fairy folk who understand
Help by giving her a hand;
They sing to her to ease her strife
And make a joy of prison life.

Caterpillars

A caterpillar small and hairy
   Is sometimes ridden by a fairy;
They treat it like a fairy horse
And tend to ride for fun of course.

   Caterpillars big and green
   Are quite the nicest I have seen;
   They blow themselves up big – it's true
   To frighten birds and people too.

Caterpillars small and thin
Go quite unnoticed – its a sin;
They hang about on leaves and eat
And have a lot of little feet.

   And caterpillars with the moon
   Wind themselves in a cocoon,
   And when the time is very right
   A lovely butterfly takes flight.

Butterfly poem

Butterflies are made of this:
  A lovely smile, a fairy's kiss,
A rainbow shining in the sky,
A fluffy cloud that passes by.

  A gift from Source that's with us still,
  With gentleness our lives to fill –
  A butterfly is perfect, free,
    Brings beauty for us all to see.

Washing day

Down in the garden
   Where the fairies live
There's such a hullaballoo!
Down in the garden
Where the fairies live
There's a really big to-do!

   It's washing day
   And all their clothes
   Were hanging on the line,
   And then a sparrow came along
   And said "Those clothes are mine!"

He took them all,
He took them all!
They can't believe it's true.
He went and took the flipping lot!
Now what are they to do?

The fairy clothes shop's ready
To have a sell-out day ...
It's just as well
She's made a lot,
They'll all be whisked away ...

... by fairies
Whose dresses
Are now up in a tree ...
Held by naughty sparrow,
Who giggles –
   Tee hee hee!

Catkin time

Little lambs' tails all a-tangle,
    In the woodland see them dangle.
Playing on the breeze they swing;
The pollen flies like anything.

  The trees must help themselves and so
  This is why the catkins grow,
  And fairies help them with delight
  To fertilise with main and might.

For fairies it's a time to treasure,
A time that's filled with endless pleasure ...
As they swing from tree to tree
Carrying pollen like a bee.

I wish I was a fairy too,
  Swinging on catkins as they do.
  With my pretty coloured wings
  I'd do a lot of lovely things.

I'd fly above the trees and flowers,
Oh I'd have many happy hours;
I'd spend them oh most usefully,
  Carrying pollen from tree to tree.

Child's Prayer

Father Mother Wakan Tanka,
  Keeper of our sacred lands,
Hear my prayer for all your creatures
  As beneath your sky I stand.

Hear my prayer that all your creatures
Free, united, may they be.
Hear my prayer for all us beings
That we may be just like thee.

  Help us all to see the vision
  Of a land that's healed and strong.
  Help us all to see a vision
  Of a time that can't go wrong.

Help us all to be the dreamers,
Dancing dreams of love awake.
Help us all to be united,
Dreaming for our planet's sake.

Father Mother Wakan Tanka
Hear my prayer however small;
It's a prayer that you will help us,
And that you will save us all.

Gnome poem

Here's a funny little poem
About a very happy gnome
Who lived beneath a big oak tree
And had boiled acorns for his tea.

He wore a suit of green and red ...
A small red hat upon his head ...
Was very rarely seen about,
And never ever heard to shout.

He looked after the oak trees' roots
And climbed them in his little boots
And talked to them about the sky
And all the birds he'd seen pass by.

The roots did thrive because you know
It is beneath the ground they grow,
And never hear about the sky,
Unless a gnome is passing by.

And so his days they were content;
He never had to pay his rent
And never had to leave his home
Unless he got the urge to roam.
(He never has and never will,
For all I know he lives there still)

So next time you are walking past
An oak tree with a bit of class
Look carefully amongst its roots
For little gnomes ...
    with small green boots.

Percy's windy day

High up on a windy hill
   A red kite in his hand,
A little mouse in jacket blue
Did make his autumn stand.

   His kite was strong with tail so long.
   The wind blew off his hat.
   His mother said "Be careful, dear"
   And stopped to have a chat.

And so he launched his mighty kite;
With easy grace it flew.
The spindle thing unwound the string,
It went quite fast 'tis true.

The wind did gust, the kite did bob
And tightened on the string.
The little mouse he held on tight
And yelled like anything!

"Mum! Mum!" he cried,
"Where are you?
The wind's too strong to stand!
My nice red kite's aloft all right
But it's hurting my poor hand."

And then a playful gust of wind
Came calling by and by,
And pulled poor Percy off his feet
And up into the sky.

continued ...

19

Just then Mrs. Mouse looked up
And saw his dangling feet.
"Oh Mum, Oh Mum! Please! Help me!"
She heard her son repeat.

"Oh help, please help!" cried Mrs. Mouse,
"I don't know what to do!
The kite has carried Percy off
And him so little too!"

A passing swallow heard her wail
And went to get more help.
They flew to help poor Percy,
And you should have heard him yelp.

The swallows brought the kite to earth
And Percy gave a sigh.
The animals all cheered the birds
For the rescue in the sky.

So Percy went on home to bed,
And when his Dad was told
He said "Hmm... I quite fancy that,
One has to be quite bold."

    And that is how hang–gliding
    Became a woodland spree,
    And ... as Percy proudly said:
       "It's all because of me!"

Bluebell time

A little bluebell fairy
   So beautiful to see
Gave her little clarion call
And danced around in glee.

   And within the bluebell woods
   The sound of tinkling chimes
   Told all the creatures of the woods
   Come! Come! It's bluebell time.

Come! Come and sit with us a while
And look at all the blue
And smell our wondrous fragrance,
And drink some of our dew.

For we are messengers from Heaven
Who've come to bring you calm
And happiness and healing
And keep you free from harm.

Our fairy friends will sing to you
And we will ring and chime
And give you peace to last you
  Till another bluebell time.

Wand practice

In the woods the fairies meet,
   In fairy rings which are so neat.
With wands aloft they practise spells
Midst lots of giggles, laughs and yells.

   They really have to get it right
   And try and try with all their might
   Not to make a daft mistake,
   For every other other creature's sake.

When "Wand Practice!" reached their ears
The other creatures disappeared,
They went to hide themselves away
To live to see another day.

If in the woods you stray by chance
And all is quiet as if in trance
A fairy giggle you may hear
Just audible to human ear.

If I were you straight home I'd go.
I wouldn't want to linger so
In case you get to truly see
    How dangerous a wand can be.

The beetle poem

There's a Beetle in the garden called Ringo,
  There are others called George
And called John.
There's another called Paul
And I know that's not all
But the others they just hum along.

  The Beetles, they play at the concerts
  That the fairies arrange in the spring;
  And at Christmas too
  They give quite a do
  And they sing and they sing and they sing.

  The dwarves, they record all the concerts
  On crystals and sell them for cakes,
  'Cos dwarves like their nosh
    And can't cook for a tosh
      So good food is all that it takes.

The Beetles are known in the garden
And in the neighbourhood too
They are in such demand
And at Royal command!
(The Fairy Queen bops to them too).

A grasshopper sometimes plays fiddle
And a few other creatures join in,
And the Fairy Queen,
Why, she plays tambourine
Whenever the Beetles all sing.

You may not believe there are beetles
Who sing in the gardens around,
But I've heard them play
On many a day
And I love the way
that they sound.

Differences

Fairies are beautiful and they fly,
   Gnomes and pixies scamper by,
Butterflies fly and dragon flies too,
But dwarves they walk like me and you.

   Fairies have wands and pixies don't,
   Fairies make spells but pixies won't,
   Dwarves like crystals
      that shimmer and shine,
   Gnomes think trees are just divine.

I love trees ...
and plants and flowers
And play in the garden
for hours and hours.

So I see the gnomes
And the pixies too
And the fairies that fly ...
I swear it's true.

They see me coming
And always say
"Hey little girl,
Please come and play!"

The brownie poem

My mother said I never could,
   see the Brownies in the wood,
But I saw the Brownies yesterday,
Playing at leap frog and I wanted to play.

   I've seen the Brownies playing at "He",
   I saw the Brownies but they didn't see me!
   I've seen them playing at Hop-Scotch too
   And the Big Ship sails in the Alley Alley oo!

Tomorrow when I go they'll all be there,
All the little Brownies jumping in the air,
      Climbing on to toadstools and
         bathing in the Sun.
            Being a Brownie must be lots
               and lots of fun

What do fairies do?

Oh little fairies as you fly
   Do you race the clouds as they pass by?
And spend your many happy hours
Smelling the fragrance of pretty flowers

And every day at half past three
Do you wash your hands in time for tea
Does the fairy Queen shout loud at four
   "Come in, come in, and close the door"

"Will I be Mum or my dear will you
   Lift up the tea-pot dear please do
   And let us all have tea and cake
   with napkins white and pretty plates"

Or do you drink the dew from leaves
And eat red berries where you please
And do you take your sweet repose
   Curled up inside a fragrant rose.

The Queen's tea

Acorn cups of lemonade,
Wobbly jellies, newly made,
White blancmange in towers light,
Little cakes with icing bright.

Sandwiches all cut in shapes,
Twigs of tiny little grapes,
Lovely ice cream in a mound,
Glowing colours all around.

For royal cheer the fairy Queen's
Expected to arrive unseen,
And hearts a-flutter, nervous though,
Go fairies flitting to and fro ...

To make sure everything's just right
For Her to take a royal bite
Of the feast that's been prepared
Showing how they've really cared.

Quick! Quick!
The call – It's Her,
It's She,
Her Majesty
has come to tea!

Elves are special

The elves have special magic
  And are very rarely seen;
When little elves come to your life
It feels just like a dream.

  For time stands still,
  And things you do
  Which seem to take two hours
  Are over in a minute –
  Just like knocking down brick towers.

I like the elves,
They cannot live
In towns like me and you,
They have to go to other worlds
And then they come back through

To talk to little boys and girls
To tell us what is right;
 Just how to help the flowers and trees
To grow their colours bright.

So that the world is full of love,
With colour everywhere,
And the little elves can come back in
And stay without a care.

The dance

"Watch!" said the breeze
    As it whisked in the trees
As breezes often do.
"Watch!" said the breeze
As it stirred a leaf,
    "Just see what I can do!"

And the spirits of the wind
All laughed for joy
    As wind sprites often do,
And they whisked through the air
With never a care
    And love for me and you.

And the sycamore trees
Reached out to the breeze
  And their small propeller seeds
Flew into the air
And played with the breeze
  And danced with the sprites with ease.

  And the dandelion clocks
  All said tick tock
    And their seeds joined in the jig;
  And the petals from the flowers
  Of a flowering tree
    Came dancing away from a twig.

continued ...

37

And Mother Nature sighed
And smiled to see
  This wondrous dance unfold
And the spirits of the wind
Took the seeds in their care
  And took them to places untold,

  And planted the seeds
  Upon the ground
    Where they could happy be
  To grow into flowers
  And trees, my dears,
    For the pleasure of you and me.

The fairy's birthday

To the sales a fairy went
    To see what she could buy;
She saw a lovely pinky dress
That really caught her eye.

    Then she went to Gossamer Spider's shop
    Across the road and round,
    And a beautiful shiny silken dress
    Of gossamer she found.

Next to Butterfly's for rings,
Bracelets, ear rings too,
And other shiny nick nacks
Which fairies love, it's true!

    Then to Moth's shop for a hat,
    The very latest kind;
    And then a shawl from Silkworm,
    The loveliest she could find.

From Cobbler Mole a pair of shoes
That fitted her a treat;
A very lovely shade of blue
They looked so very neat.

And finally, all kitted out,
A tiny bag did sit
Upon her little shoulder
With her handkerchief in it.

And now the little fairy
In her new clothes so divine
Went to her birthday party
And her birthday turned out fine.

The magic people

The magic people are here.
    They came in gently
Like thistledown upon the breeze;
They did not come
In a rush and bustle,
They came in – silent as the trees.

The magic people are here.
They came in with love,
Which enfolds us gently
Like a warm soft sea;
They haven't come to hurry us
They've come to help and let us be.

The magic people are here.
They're golden and warm
Just like the sun that shines in the day;
They love us so it is all right,
They're here ...
And they won't go away.

The celebration

On a summer's evening, it was June,
  When the fullness shone from sister Moon
There was a woodland celebration
You could only go by invitation.

  The Grasshopper String Quartet was there
  And played and played with never a care
  And the creatures waltzed the night away
  Until the dawning of the day.

Butterflies, elves and fairies light
Moles and voles and fireflies bright,
Glow worms! Glow worms all a–glister
Dancing for the moon, their sister.

    Golden angels danced above
    Sending down their rays of love
    Upon the fairy celebration,
    Dancing waltzes in formation.

My helpers

Lovely white angels
  With wings of light
Come to see me
In bed at night.

  They show me pictures
  Of beautiful places
  And shiny people
  With lovely faces.

And then they sing me
Such beautiful songs;
And I fall asleep,
And it doesn't take long.

And while I'm sleeping
They stay with me still
So that when I wake up
I'm with happiness filled.

What I found

In the garden yesterday
A little stick I found
With a shining, silver star on top
That sparkled all around.

It really was quite beautiful,
It took my breath away.
I wondered where it came from,
How it came to me that day.

Just then a butterly flew by
And stopped to say "Hello"
She gave a little curtsey
And she flew a little low.

48

"Why, you have found the fairy's wand"
I heard the creature say.
"She's been crying since she lost it
So shout 'Hip Hip Hip Hurray'".

So I gave it to the butterfly
Who took it on her way
To return it to the fairy
Who had had a horrid day.

And as I sat there wondering
A small voice called to me
And I saw a little fairy
As lovely as can be.

"I am so glad you found my wand,
I missed it so", said she.
"Would you like to come to Fairy Land
And have a special tea?"

continued ...

And so I went with Fairy Fay
The fairy folk to see,
And the tea it was so scrumptious
And the fairies sang to me.

There were sandwiches of petal jam
And wobbly jelly too
And little plates of honeycomb,
Which was delicious too.

And acorn cups of lemonade
And tea in little cups,
And the fairies all said "thank you",
And "won't you drink it up".

And then I got quite sleepy
And I curled up by a tree,
And when I woke they all had gone;
T'was like a dream to me.

    I looked round for my little friends
    But it wasn't any good,
    The magic time had come and gone
    And left me where I stood.

And as I sadly looked around
I saw beside the tree
A tiny little parcel
Which I knew was just for me.

continued ...

And there within the parcel
A tiny little ring
For me to wear on special days
When I go visiting.

'Cos always when I put it on
It brings the fairies close;
And I know that I can visit them
Just when I want to most.

So I keep it in a little box
And at night while I'm asleep
It's there beneath my pillow
Where my precious things I keep.

My Angel

There's an Angel who stands
  by my bed at night,
All lovely and shiny
  and dressed in white;
And if I close my eyes it doesn't go away
My Angel tells me that it's going to stay.

The Angel by my bed says
  "Do not be alarmed!
For I am your Guardian
  and will keep you free from harm";
And then I know that the Love I feel
  Coming from my Angel is very
    very real.

And I say:
    "Mummy I have got
        an Angel near"
And she says "Don't be silly!"
    or pretends she cannot hear.
But I've got an Angel and
    I know, I know, I know,
That my Angel is real
    and will never never go.

And even when I'm big
    it will always be around,
To help me and keep me safe
    with never any sound;
And if I choose to see it then
    I'll not be round the bend,
And my Angel will stay with me
    and be my friend.

Terry needs a home

I know a Gnome who needs a home,
  He's very clean and neat.
And when he comes in from outside
He always wipes his feet.

  He loves to do the drying up
  And goes to bed quite early.
  He has a tiny little beard
  That's black and rather curly.

He'll wash and iron the clothes for you

And put the kettle on,
And put the cat out for the night
And sing a gnomey song.

  He needs a place where he can stay
  And mostly he loves trees.
  He'll sing to them and nurture them
  And do anything to please.

So can you find a home for him?
He says his name is Terry.
If you take a gnome into your home
  Your life is always merry.

Lullaby

Hush, my dear;
  Little birds in their nests
Are closing their sleepy eyes.
Hush, my dear,
For the angels so bright
Are watching on you from the skies.

And all the little creatures
Are curling up so small.
And all the horses, children too
Are sleeping in their stall.

Hush, my dear;
Be not afraid,
Come lay your sleepy head
On pillows that are soft and cool,
Like clouds upon your bed.

And dream of rainbows,
Little one,
As children often do;
For fairy-folk and angels, dear,
Are watching over you.

*I would like to thank the fairies and the spirits of the
ancestors for their part in bringing together this book.*